P9-CLF-406

Table of Contents

HOW TO USE THIS BOOK

1 Sit around with a bunch of friends.

2 Read a question from this book out loud and talk about it. You won't believe some of the stuff you'll come up with as you think about which choice to make.

3 Everybody must choose! That's the whole point. It forces you to really think about the options.

4 Once everyone has chosen, move on to the next question.

It's that simple. We have provided a few things to think about for each question, but don't stop there. Much of the fun comes from imagining the different ways your choice will affect your life.

You may want to grab a pencil, as sometimes you will get to fill in the blank with someone you know or other information. Other times, you will make up your own questions, keep score of who chose what, and more!

Enough jibber-jabber. It's time to enter the wacky world of *Would You Rather...?*

WOULD YOU RATHER...?

Over 300 crazy questions plus extra pages to make up your own!

Gross-Out

Justin Heimberg & David Gomberg

Published by Seven Footer Press
276 Fifth Ave., Suite 301
New York, NY 10001

First Printing, November 2008
10 9 8 7 6 5 4 3

Would you rather...?® is a registered trademark used under license
from Falls Media LLC, an Imagination company

Design by Tom Schirtz

ISBN-13 978-1-934734-35-3

ii

Chapter One

Gross!

Here's the deal: For reasons beyond your understanding, your life is about to change. That fascination you have with vomit, vermin, boogers, and bugs is about to come back to haunt you. You wanted gross, you got it. You are given a choice between two possible fates, each delightfully more disgusting than the next.

Would you rather...

swallow five live cockroaches

OR

have to bathe for a week in a tub filled to the brim with octopuses?

Would you rather...

chew on toe cheese **OR** ear wax?

a leaf of poison ivy **OR** a piece of gum you found on the bottom of your shoe?

a regurgitated cat hair-ball **OR** a booger the size of a marble?

YOU MUST CHOOSE!

WOULD YOU RATHER... HAVE HAIRY GUMS

OR ANTS CRAWLING IN YOUR ARMPITS?

Would you rather...

brush your teeth with mashed slug toothpaste

OR

blow your nose using a stranger's used tissue?

Reasons 1st choice is better   Reasons 2nd choice is better

_____   _____

_____   _____

_____   _____

Would you rather...

have to eat a snotsicle

OR

a roadkill hot dog?

YOU MUST CHOOSE!

4

Would you rather...

stick a straw into a termite mound and suck up termites for one minute

OR

sleep a night in a bed filled with used kitty litter?

Reasons 1st choice is better

_____

_____

_____

Reasons 2nd choice is better

_____

_____

_____

Gross!

YOU MUST CHOOSE!

Fill in the Blank!
Would you rather...

only be able to eat _____ for the rest
(insert awful tasting food)
of your life

OR

have to wear the clothes of _____
(insert person who
_____ each day after he/she wears
never bathes)
them?

YOU MUST CHOOSE!

Would you rather...

wear clothes made out of sopping wet seaweed

OR

vomit five baby frogs each time you wake up?

YOU MUST CHOOSE!

Would you rather...

have night crawler worms come out whenever you sneeze

OR

step in dog poop once a day for the rest of your life?

YOU MUST CHOOSE!

Gross Out

Would you rather...

be limited to drinking the pus from popped pimples for a week

OR

have your shower/bath water replaced with rhinoceros urine?

Take a vote!

Number of people who voted for choice #1: _____

Number of people who voted for choice #2: _____

YOU MUST CHOOSE!

Make Your Own "Gross" Question!
Make up two choices that are equally gross!

Would you rather....

_____

_____

OR

_____

_____ ?

Who chose what...

Name _____

Choice _____

Name _____

Choice _____

YOU MUST CHOOSE!

Gross!

11

Would you rather...

have an inch of flimsy extra skin at the end of your fingers like gloves that are too big

OR

have three inches of extra skin at the end of your nose?

YOU MUST CHOOSE!

Would you rather...

drink a bowl of soup cooked with toilet water broth in a pot filled with used retainers

OR

lick the eye gunk out of your classmates' eyes?

Gross!

YOU MUST CHOOSE!

13

Would you rather...

permanently share your bedroom with 1,000 mosquitoes **OR** 5 boa constrictors?

25 black widow spiders **OR** 3 pits filled with quicksand?

a gassy Bigfoot **OR** an elephant with allergies?

YOU MUST CHOOSE!

Would you rather...

have dandelions for hair **OR** strands of cooked spaghetti?

dangerous electric wire **OR** centipedes?

tree branches **OR** tentacles?

YOU MUST CHOOSE!

Would you rather...

suck every drop of sweat from the socks of the Dallas Cowboys after a game

OR

eat a sandwich wrap made from shedded snake-skin filled with a mixture of fingernail clippings?

Would you rather...

suck on a sheep's eyeball

OR

a cow's tongue?

Gross!

YOU MUST CHOOSE!

WOULD YOU RATHER...HAVE TO WASH YOUR FACE EVERYDAY IN A HEAVILY POPULATED BIRD BATH

OR HAVE TO BRUSH YOUR TEETH EACH DAY WITH TWO YEAR OLD NACHO CHEESE?

Would you rather...

eat a grilled cheese covered in maggots

OR

a caramel apple rolled on the floor of a barber shop?

Gross!

YOU MUST CHOOSE!

Would you rather...
produce poops that wriggle and squirm like snakes upon falling in the toilet

OR

be able to fart the tune of "Breaking Free" from *High School Musical*?

Would you rather...
permanently house a family of crickets in your pants

OR

have to use the same Band-Aid for the rest of your life?

YOU MUST CHOOSE!

Gross Out

Would you rather...
gargle quick-drying cement mouthwash
OR
inhale Krazy glue nasal spray?

Take a vote!

Number of people who voted for choice #1: _____

Number of people who voted for choice #2: _____

Gross!

YOU MUST CHOOSE!

21

Would you rather...

only be able to wear clothes that are infested with fleas

OR

live inside the hull of a garbage truck?

Take a vote!

Number of people who voted for choice #1: _____

Number of people who voted for choice #2: _____

YOU MUST CHOOSE!

Would you rather...

have a sleep disorder that causes you to burp uncontrollably as you sleep instead of snore

OR

only be able to talk with other people when your eyelids are flipped inside out?

Gross!

YOU MUST CHOOSE!

Would you rather...

take a bite out of a pita filled with dragonflies

OR

dunk your head into a bucket of monkey brains?

Would you rather...

sweat maple syrup

or

cry grape jelly?

YOU MUST CHOOSE!

Would you rather...

have to always wear a pair of used underwear on your head as a hat

OR

never be able to flush a toilet?

Reasons 1st choice is better

Reasons 2nd choice is better

_____

_____

_____

_____

_____

_____

Gross!

YOU MUST CHOOSE!

25

Would you rather...

be thrown up on by six giraffes

OR

force an entire hotdog up your nose?

YOU MUST CHOOSE!

Would you rather...

wear shoes that are always filled with fudge **OR** ice?

ketchup **OR** rocks?

scorpions **OR** sewing needles?

_____ **OR** _____?
(insert your own)   (insert your own)

Gross!

YOU MUST CHOOSE!

Would you rather...

eat a piece of cake that had a 50% chance of having a dead mouse in the middle

OR

grab and eat a handful of M&M's with one third of those M&M's actually being fish eyes?

YOU MUST CHOOSE!

Would you rather...

eat a scoop of ice cream out of an old dirty shoe

OR

eat a salad sprinkled with boogers?

Take a vote!

Number of people who voted for choice #1: _____

Number of people who voted for choice #2: _____

Gross!

YOU MUST CHOOSE!

Would you rather...

have no furniture in your house

OR

have no toilet in your house?

YOU MUST CHOOSE!

Would you rather...
lick your friend's chicken pox
OR
use Tabasco sauce eye drops?

Gross!

YOU MUST CHOOSE!

Chapter Two

You've Been Cursed

You are about to suffer a terrible curse—something that will change your life forever in all sorts of ways. Luckily for you, there is a silver lining to this dark cloud. You get to choose between two possible fates.

YOU MUST CHOOSE!

Would you rather...

have a cow's udder on your stomach

OR

a turkey neck with lots of skin hanging down?

Would you rather...

only be able to hear words spoken by females

OR

upon hitting the age of 60, slowly turn into a salmon?

YOU MUST CHOOSE!

35

Would you rather...

gain 50 pounds between the hours of 11AM and 2PM every day, returning to your normal weight again after 2PM

OR

lose 10 pieces of hair which will never grow back for every minute you're exposed to sunlight?

Things to think about: lunchroom sumo

YOU MUST CHOOSE!

Would you rather...

have fingernails that grow at a rate of one inch per minute

OR

have eyebrows that grow at the same rate?

Would you rather...

add "De" to the front of your first name

OR

insert a silent "b" into your name wherever you want?

YOU MUST CHOOSE!

Would you rather...

have glow-in-the-dark veins

OR

be able to watch only one television show for the rest of your life: *Dora the Explorer*?

Reasons 1st choice is better | Reasons 2nd choice is better

_____ | _____

_____ | _____

_____ | _____

YOU MUST CHOOSE!

Would you rather...

have 2 tongues **OR** 20 toes?

nostrils scattered all over your face **OR** no nostrils?

arms as long as your entire body **OR** a head shaped exactly like a football (including seams/stitches)?

YOU MUST CHOOSE!

WOULD YOU RATHER...HAVE 20 INCH NOSTRIL HAIR

OR 20 INCH LONG TOENAILS?

BOING!

WOULD YOU RATHER...?

40

Would you rather...

suck in air with the force of a vacuum when yawning

OR

have blow-dryer strength farts?

Take a vote!

Number of people who voted for choice #1: _____

Number of people who voted for choice #2: _____

YOU MUST CHOOSE!

Would you rather...

have steel fingernails **OR** anti-gravity earlobes?

skateboards for feet **OR** paintbrushes for hands?

Stegosaurus spikes along your spine **OR** an anteater snout?

YOU MUST CHOOSE!

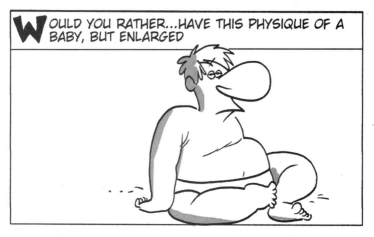

WOULD YOU RATHER...HAVE THIS PHYSIQUE OF A BABY, BUT ENLARGED

OR HAVE VELCRO BODY HAIR?

Would you rather...

have your name legally changed to

Doo Doo Franklin **OR** Farty Fart Johnson?

Smelvin **OR** Anita Bath?

Make up your own names: _____

OR _____ ?

Would you rather...

have Slinkys for arms

OR

Silly Putty for skin?

Things to think about: _____

_____

_____

YOU MUST CHOOSE!

Make Your Own "You've Been Cursed" Question!

Would you rather....

_____

_____

OR

_____

_____ ?

Who chose what...

Name _____

Choice _____

Name _____

Choice _____

YOU MUST CHOOSE!

Would you rather...

have to wear underwear made from spider webs (the spiders are still living in the webs)

OR

be permanently chained to one of your brothers/sisters?

Would you rather...

only be able to open your eyes 1/8th of an inch

OR

only be able to open your mouth 1/8th of an inch?

Things to think about: eating, bad Karaoke

YOU MUST CHOOSE!

47

Would you rather...
only be able to wear yellow clothing

OR

have to use a flounder for a wallet?

Would you rather...
have sand for blood

OR

saltwater for saliva?

YOU MUST CHOOSE!

You've Been Cursed

Would you rather...

have everything you say come out as a question?

OR

your have the random sentence in out come order?

Would you rather...

have chicken pox that you can peel off and eat like Candy Buttons

OR

have chocolate boogers?

YOU MUST CHOOSE!

Would you rather...

have pockets filled with an infinite supply of Gummi Bears but be incapable of speaking when not wearing a headband and matching wristbands

OR

have near-perfect knowledge of computer programming but on Fridays become convinced you are a glass of orange juice and desperately struggle not to spill yourself?

YOU MUST CHOOSE!

OULD YOU RATHER...HAVE A NECK AS LONG AS YOUR TORSO

R A TORSO AS SHORT AS YOUR NECK?

Fill in the Blank!
Would you rather always have to wear...

pants made of _____
(insert material)

OR

socks made of _____?
(insert animal fur)

Would you rather...

be invisible to your parents on Sundays

OR

have stalks of broccoli sprout from various spots on your body whenever you get nervous?

Things to think about: Presenting in front of your class, talking to the person you have a crush on

YOU MUST CHOOSE!

Would you rather...

only gain weight on the top half of your body

OR

only gain weight on the left side of your body?

Things to think about: Career as a wrestler named Asymmetrical McGee

Take a vote!

Number of people who voted for choice #1: _____

Number of people who voted for choice #2: _____

YOU MUST CHOOSE!

WOULD YOU RATHER...HAVE BENDY STRAWS FOR HAIR

OR NEWSPAPER FOR SKIN?

Would you rather...

walk through all doorways as if you were in the middle of an intense limbo competition

OR

have a strange to desire to always make a hula hoop motion whenever you're in the presence of your school principal?

Reasons 1st choice is better

_____

_____

_____

Reasons 2nd choice is better

_____

_____

_____

YOU MUST CHOOSE!

WOULD YOU RATHER...?

Would you rather...
be the size of an ant
OR
of a blue whale?

Who chose what...

Name _____

Choice _____

Name _____

Choice _____

Would you rather...
fart out of your nose
OR
pee through your belly button?

YOU MUST CHOOSE!

Would you rather...
have cleats built into your feet

OR
have miniature ivory elephant tusks on your face?

Reasons 1st choice is better

_____

_____

_____

Reasons 2nd choice is better

_____

_____

_____

YOU MUST CHOOSE!

Would you rather...
always have to wear a 20 lb. necklace
OR
swimming goggles?

Things to think about: _____

_____

_____

_____

_____

_____

YOU MUST CHOOSE!

Would you rather...

have an Adam's apple the size of a watermelon

OR

have feet as long as you are tall?

Things to think about: Toppling forward

Take a vote!

Number of people who voted for choice #1: _____

Number of people who voted for choice #2: _____

YOU MUST CHOOSE!

Would you rather...

have to answer your teacher's questions by rapping your answers

OR

by miming them?

Would you rather...

have to eat anything handed to you within 3 seconds of receiving it

OR

be incapable of standing in one place for more than 3 seconds without starting to melt?

YOU MUST CHOOSE!

Chapter Three

Powers and Fantasies

It's your luck day. You are about to be blessed with a magical superpower to rival Superman, Spider-man, and Iron Man. Even better, you have a say in the matter. You get to choose between two options.

Would you rather...

have the power to shoot dental floss from your fingertips

OR

have a working thermometer going up your shin?

Would you rather...

be able to blow gum bubbles capable of lifting you into the air like a hot air balloon

OR

have the power to make any food taste like any other food?

Things to think about: What food would you want you want your food to taste like?

YOU MUST CHOOSE!

Would you rather...

have Wii controls that work for real people in front of you (voodoo style)

OR

have every fortune in your fortune cookies become true?

Reasons 1st choice is better   Reasons 2nd choice is better

_____   _____

_____   _____

_____   _____

YOU MUST CHOOSE!

WOULD YOU RATHER...HAVE A HEAD THAT REFLECTS LIGHT LIKE A DISCO PARTY BALL

OR PUFF UP LIKE A BLOWFISH WHEN YOU SENSE DANGER?

Would you rather...

be able to speak to cats if it meant you had to use a litter box when you needed to go the bathroom

OR

be able to speak to dogs if it meant you had to greet your friends by sniffing them?

Who chose what and why...

Name _____ Choice _____

Why _____

Name _____ Choice _____

Why _____

YOU MUST CHOOSE!

Powers and Fantasies

67

Would you rather...

have a Disney Channel musical based on your life

OR

have Domino's name a new type of pizza after you?

Things to think about: What would you name that pizza?

Fill in the Blank!
Would you rather...

be able to see through all _____

(insert object)

OR

be able to spray _____
from your nostrils?

(insert liquid)

YOU MUST CHOOSE!

Would you rather...

have a permanent hot chocolate aftertaste
OR
be capable of shifting the features of your face around like a Mr. Potato Head?

Things to think about: Draw a picture below of how you would arrange your face.

YOU MUST CHOOSE!

Would you rather...

have the ability to produce blistering sunburns on other people by staring at them

OR

the power to produce frostbite with your breath?

Things to think about: Would you use your power for good or evil?

YOU MUST CHOOSE!

Would you rather...

be able to sense farts 30 seconds before they happen (like a Spidey-sense)

OR

never lose a thumb-wrestling contest?

YOU MUST CHOOSE!

Would you rather...

have the power to spray a super stinky musk from scent glands on your butt like a skunk

OR

the ability to surround yourself with a cloud of ink like a squid?

YOU MUST CHOOSE!

Would you rather...

have hair that can harden into a helmet at your command

OR

be capable of producing actual musical notes when you air guitar?

Reasons 1st choice is better   Reasons 2nd choice is better

_____   _____

_____   _____

_____   _____

YOU MUST CHOOSE!

WOULD YOU RATHER...HAVE RETRACTABLE CLAWS

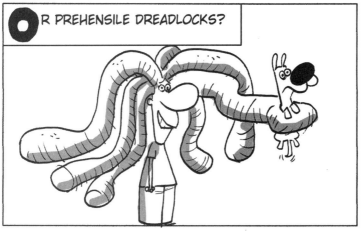

OR PREHENSILE DREADLOCKS?

Would you rather never get...

a zit **OR** a stomach ache?

embarrassed **OR** lonely?

a bad grade in school **OR** a bad birthday gift from your friends and family?

Would you rather...

be able to cool soup to a perfect temperature with merely one blow

OR

be able to neaten sloppy joes by concentrating hard?

YOU MUST CHOOSE!

Make Your Own "Powers" Question!
Would you rather have the power to...

_____

_____

OR

_____

_____ **?**

Who chose what...

Name _____

Choice _____

Name _____

Choice _____

YOU MUST CHOOSE!

WOULD YOU RATHER...YOUR BELLY BUTTON DOUBLE AS AN ELECTRIC OUTLET

OR BE ABLE TO SWAP YOUR FACE AT WILL WITH ANYONE ELSE?

Would you rather...

be able to download songs from iTunes directly into your head

OR

have complete knowledge of what is on TV at any given time?

YOU MUST CHOOSE!

Would you rather...

be able to cause lactose intolerance in people by shaking hands with them

OR

be capable of causing motion sickness in people by singing to them?

Reasons 1st choice is better

_____

_____

_____

Reasons 2nd choice is better

_____

_____

_____

YOU MUST CHOOSE!

Would you rather...

have a toothbrush built into your index finger

OR

a hair brush built into the palm of your hand?

Take a vote!

Number of people who voted for choice #1: _____

Number of people who voted for choice #2: _____

YOU MUST CHOOSE!

WOULD YOU RATHER...HAVE A DETACHABLE FU MANCHU MUSTACHE/BOOMERANG

ZING

VOOP!

OR "THRUSTERS ON THE BOTTOMS OF YOUR FEET?

ZOOM!

Would you rather...
be able to spit globs of phlegm 50 feet with 100% accuracy

OR

have the power to summon background singers at any moment by snapping your fingers?

Would you rather...
drool Pepsi

OR

have rose-scented sweat?

YOU MUST CHOOSE!

Would you rather...

be able to write with perfect penmanship using your feet

OR

be able to speak fluent Pig Latin?

Things to think about: Wearing flip-flops to school

Would you rather...

have the power to see in the dark

OR

be capable of breathing fire like a dragon?

Things to think about: How about if you could only use your power to light barbeques?

YOU MUST CHOOSE!

Would you rather spend the day with...

the Jonas Brothers **OR** LeBron James?

Will Smith **OR** Drake Bell?

the real-life incarnations of characters from *Harry Potter* **OR** the real-life incarnations of characters from *Lord of the Rings*?

Things to think about: Who would you most want to spend the day with?

YOU MUST CHOOSE!

Would you rather...

provided no one can watch, be able to jump 100 feet up into the air

OR

have the ability to run 40 miles per hour?

YOU MUST CHOOSE!

Would you rather...
have the ability to hold your breath indefinitely

OR

be able to stop time?

Reasons 1st choice is better

Reasons 2nd choice is better

_____   _____

_____   _____

_____   _____

YOU MUST CHOOSE!

Would you rather...

be able to fold yourself completely in half
OR
have the power to perfectly fillet fish with your pinkies?

Take a vote!

Number of people who voted for choice #1: _____

Number of people who voted for choice #2: _____

YOU MUST CHOOSE!

Would you rather...

be able to always accurately predict the next word that will be spoken to you

OR

be able to keep any piece of fruit from spoiling by dropping it down your pants?

YOU MUST CHOOSE!

Chapter Four

Cool and Unusual Punishments

Uh oh. You must have done something wrong. Because the fates have decided that you must suffer a horrible experience—a painful challenge, an embarrassing moment, or something else horrific, disgusting, or just generally unpleasant.

Would you rather...

be caught in an avalanche of horse dung

OR

a tidal wave of dog slobber?

Would you rather...

get hit in the eye with the juice of a popped zit

OR

get hit in the mouth with the guts of a squashed caterpillar?

YOU MUST CHOOSE!

Would you rather...

find out that all of your moments in front of a mirror in the past week have been secretly filmed and will be shown to your school during an assembly

OR

that all of your conversations with friends for the past week have been recorded and will be broadcast on your local radio?

Reasons 1st choice is better

_____

_____

_____

Reasons 2nd choice is better

_____

_____

_____

YOU MUST CHOOSE!

WOULD YOU RATHER...HAVE TO WEAR CLOTHES FIVE SIZES TOO SMALL

OR HAVE TO WEAR ARTICLES OF CLOTHING ON A DIFFERENT PART OF THE BODY THAN THEY WERE INTENDED FOR?

Would you rather...

brush your teeth and gums with steel wool

OR

use recycled shampoo that was just rinsed off of a pack of pigs that had been rolling in the mud?

Take a vote!

Number of people who voted for choice #1: _____

Number of people who voted for choice #2: _____

YOU MUST CHOOSE!

Would you rather...

only be able to get around by skipping **OR** galloping?

doing the crabwalk **OR** crawling on your hands and knees?

by riding a unicycle **OR** by using cross-country skis?

by hopping on a pogo stick **OR** using a hang glider?

YOU MUST CHOOSE!

Would you rather...

have to dress identically to your teacher for a week

OR

identically to your mother for a week?

Who chose what and why...

Name _____ Choice _____

Why _____

Name _____ Choice _____

Why _____

YOU MUST CHOOSE!

WOULD YOU RATHER...FIGHT 3 POSSESSED LAWN MOWERS

OR THE CHARACTERS FROM SPONGEBOB SQUAREPANTS?

Would you rather...

sharpen your index finger in a pencil sharpener

OR

stick your tongue in a pot of boiling water?

What are the 5 most painful things that ever happened to you?

_____

_____

_____

_____

_____

YOU MUST CHOOSE!

Would you rather...

have all your eye blinks last 10 seconds

OR

have all your yawns last 2 hours?

Who chose what and why...

Name _____ Choice _____

Why _____

Name _____ Choice _____

Why _____

YOU MUST CHOOSE!

Make Your Own Question!
Make up two choices that are equally painful!

Would you rather....

_____

_____

OR

_____

_____ **?**

Who chose what...

Name _____

Choice _____

Name _____

Choice _____

YOU MUST CHOOSE!

Would you rather...

have to keep 20 mosquitoes in your mouth for ten minutes

OR

take a bath for ten minutes in a tub with a poisonous jellyfish?

Take a vote!

Number of people who voted for choice #1: _____

Number of people who voted for choice #2: _____

YOU MUST CHOOSE!

GrossOut

103

Would you rather...

experience a life-long atomic wedgie
OR
a life-long Indian burn?

Would you rather...

have a severe allergy to TV **OR** the telephone?

to soap **OR** to paper?

to anyone named Jon **OR** to the letter "Z"?

Things to think about: What if you were allergic to all these things? How would that affect your life?

YOU MUST CHOOSE!

Would you rather be completely convinced...

that your shadow is out to get you **OR** that your blanket is?

that your belly button is sinking deeper and deeper into your body and will eventually leave a hole through your entire body **OR** that your hair is trying to fly away?

that your uncle is Bigfoot **OR** that the remote control is a baby?

YOU MUST CHOOSE!

Would you rather...

have to plug yourself into an electrical outlet every few hours to recharge before you shut down like a laptop computer

OR

become less bright like a computer monitor low on battery as the day goes on?

Would you rather...

perpetually experience a noogie on your head

OR

have your left leg always be asleep?

YOU MUST CHOOSE!

Would you rather...
see the world in X-box 360 graphic quality
OR
hear all conversations like you were on a cell phone with spotty reception?

Reasons 1st choice is better   Reasons 2nd choice is better

_____   _____

_____   _____

_____   _____

YOU MUST CHOOSE!

Would you rather...
hole punch the skin between your thumb and pointer finger

OR

staple your earlobe to the side of your head?

Things to think about: Owwww!

Would you rather...
remove your two front teeth with a bottle opener

OR

dunk your hand in a bucket of pottery glaze and place that hand in a hot kiln?

YOU MUST CHOOSE!

Fill in the Blank!
Would you rather...
be attached at the knees with

_____
(insert someone you find annoying)

OR

have to do anything _____
tells you to do? (insert someone horrible)

YOU MUST CHOOSE!

Would you rather battle...

the Power Rangers **OR** the Teenage Mutant Ninja Turtles?

2,000 lobsters **OR** one giant Grover?

a rabid Clifford the Big Red Dog **OR** 90 Flat Stanleys?

a rhino **OR** all 43 Presidents of the United States?

YOU MUST CHOOSE!

Grossout

Would you rather...
stick your tongue in a lobster's claw
OR
dive headfirst into a thorn bush?

Would you rather...
lick a cube of dry ice
OR
have a sip of boiling water?

YOU MUST CHOOSE!

Would you rather...

always be followed by a cloud that constantly released a warm drizzle

OR

have to always peel off your scabs as soon as they form?

YOU MUST CHOOSE!

Would you rather...

spend a night in a cemetery

OR

spend a night at the beach buried in the sand up to your neck?

Would you rather...

eat a 4-inch piece of honeycomb covered in bees

OR

papier-mâché your entire body?

YOU MUST CHOOSE!

Would you rather...

fight 100 bullfrogs

OR

a ninja who is also looking for his keys at the time?

Would you rather...

sit on a toilet filled with snapping turtles

OR

one with a seat that gives off a low-voltage electrical shock?

YOU MUST CHOOSE!

Chapter Five

Grosser than Gross!

Just when you thought it was safe to eat comes another chapter about the downright dirty and disgusting. Once again, you are given a choice between two possible fates, each more ridiculously revolting than the next. So what exactly is grosser than gross? You're about to find out.

Would you rather...

lie down in a bath of bloodworms

OR

shower in cow mucus?

Would you rather...

stick your tongue in the hole of a bowling ball at the bowling alley

OR

lick the bottom and inside of a rented bowling shoe?

YOU MUST CHOOSE!

Would you rather...

have scent glands on the bottom of your feet

OR

have barnacles all over your body?

Take a vote!

Number of people who voted for choice #1: _____

Number of people who voted for choice #2: _____

YOU MUST CHOOSE!

Would you rather...

eat cookies with dead flies for chocolate chips

OR

eat an ice cream cone with 100 living ants as sprinkles?

Reasons 1st choice is better

_____

_____

_____

Reasons 2nd choice is better

_____

_____

_____

YOU MUST CHOOSE!

WOULD YOU RATHER...?

WOULD YOU RATHER...DRINK A BIG GULP OF SWEAT WRUNG OUT FROM NBA PLAYERS' UNDERGARMETS

OR A BOWL OF ICE-COLD SALIVA TOPPED WITH FLOSS RESIDUE COLLECTED OVER TEN YEARS FROM BRITISH HOMELESS MEN'S TEETH?

121

Make Your Own "Gross" Question!

Make up two choices that are equally gross!

Would you rather....

_____

_____

OR

_____

_____ **?**

Who chose what...

Name _____

Choice _____

Name _____

Choice _____

YOU MUST CHOOSE!

Would you rather...

slather mustard all over your face like suntan lotion

OR

work it through your hair like hair gel?

Would you rather...

have holes throughout your skin like Swiss cheese

OR

have a neck that inflates and deflates with your breath like a frog's throat?

Things to think about: The cost of Band-Aids, wearing scarves in the summer

More things to think about: _____

_____

YOU MUST CHOOSE!

Would you rather...

clean a bicycle wheel with your tongue

OR

take a meal from a baby's potty?

Would you rather...

spend 10 minutes in a pool filled with waterbugs

OR

rats? How about rabid Trix the Rabbit clones?

YOU MUST CHOOSE!

Would you rather...

make farts that smell like roses **OR** chocolate?

burnt toast **OR** cigar smoke?

mint **OR** bubblegum?

curry **OR** rotten meat?

What's the grossest thing you ever smelled? _____

YOU MUST CHOOSE!

Would you rather...

have a slow dripping bloody nose that never stops

OR

a persistent case of the runs?

Reasons 1st choice is better | Reasons 2nd choice is better

_____ | _____

_____ | _____

_____ | _____

YOU MUST CHOOSE!

Would you rather...

only be able to eat monkey brain **OR**
fried tarantulas?

chocolate-covered pigs' feet **OR**
barbequed alligator snout?

scorpion tails **OR**
boiled bat heads?

YOU MUST CHOOSE!

Would you rather...

have to eat all your meals from what you find in a garbage dump

OR

sleep each night in a porto-potty?

YOU MUST CHOOSE!

Grosser than Gross!

Would you rather...

produce helium-filled poops **OR** dynamite-filled poops?

perfectly cubed poops **OR** isosceles triangle-shaped poops?

poops that fade away in two minutes **OR** poops that change color depending on your mood?

YOU MUST CHOOSE!

Fill in the Blank!
Would you rather...
have to kiss a _____

(insert animal)

for 20 seconds

OR gargle with _____

(insert non-water liquid)

for 20 seconds?

Would you rather...
suck on the toes of a chimpanzee

OR

have a skunk spray its stench straight into your nostrils?

YOU MUST CHOOSE!

WOULD YOU RATHER...EAT A STICK OF COTTON CANDY ENTIRELY MADE FROM BELLY BUTTON LINT

OR DRINK A MILKSHAKE MADE FROM ST. BERNARD SLOBBER?

Would you rather...

consume, in one sitting,
300 Three Musketeers bars

OR

50 hard boiled eggs?

How many of each of these have you eaten in one sitting:

Amount

_____ pieces of pizza

_____ hot dogs

_____ Gummi bears

_____ You name the food:_____

YOU MUST CHOOSE!

Would you rather...

be limited to eating whatever you can pick
from your nose as the only source
of your daily nutrition

OR

only have one "spice" to sprinkle on your
food: freshly clipped nose hair?

YOU MUST CHOOSE!

WOULD YOU RATHER... SIT IN THE BACK SEAT WITH YOUR HEAD OUT THE WINDOW BEHIND A SLOBBERING BULLDOG SITTING IN THE FRONT SEAT WITH ITS HEAD OUT THE WINDOW...

OR WALK A NATURE TRAIL BEHIND A GASSY DONKEY?

135

Would you rather...
poop through your ears
OR
hear with your butt?

Who chose what and why...

Name _____ Choice _____

Why _____

Name _____ Choice _____

Why _____

YOU MUST CHOOSE!

WOULD YOU RATHER...
HAVE TO SWIM ACROSS A LAKE OF OATMEAL

OR EAT OATMEAL EVERY DAY FOR A YEAR?

Chapter Six

Would You Rather Live in a World Where...

This time it's the world, not you, that's changing. It could be for the better or it could be for the worse. But any way you slice it, the laws of nature are about to be turned upside-down. And the best part is that you get to decide how!

Would you rather live in a world...

where it rained root beer

OR

where it snowed cheese puffs?

Take a vote!

Number of people who voted for choice #1: _____

Number of people who voted for choice #2: _____

YOU MUST CHOOSE!

Would you rather live in a world...

where a 50 mph wind blew upwards

OR

downwards?

Reasons 1st choice is better

_____

_____

_____

Reasons 2nd choice is better

_____

_____

_____

YOU MUST CHOOSE!

Would you rather live in a world...

where people used live animals as house furniture

OR

where running water was replaced with pickle juice?

YOU MUST CHOOSE!

Would you rather live in a world...

where people sniffed each other like dogs when they met

OR

where they charged each other like rams when angry at each other?

YOU MUST CHOOSE!

Would you rather live in a world...

where each day you woke up with a random new hairstyle

OR

where each day you woke up in a different part of the world?

YOU MUST CHOOSE!

Would you rather...

go to a school where you were graded on video game skills

OR

how funny you are when making fun of the teacher?

YOU MUST CHOOSE!

Would you rather live in a world...

where your height changed each day

OR

your name did?

Reasons 1st choice is better

_____

_____

_____

Reasons 2nd choice is better

_____

_____

_____

YOU MUST CHOOSE!

Would you rather live in a world...

where all foods that were bad for you became good for you

OR

where all arguments with your parents were settled with dodgeball contests?

Would you rather live in a world without...

ice cream **OR** vegetables?

baseball **OR** snow?

cartoons **OR** music?

_____ **OR** _____ ?

(insert anything)   (insert anything)

YOU MUST CHOOSE!

Would you rather live in a world...

where it always smelled like decaying meat

OR

where there was always the sound of babies crying?

Reasons 1st choice is better   Reasons 2nd choice is better

_____   _____

_____   _____

_____   _____

YOU MUST CHOOSE!

Would you rather live in a world...

where you are only able to speak with words in alphabetical order (each word must come later alphabetically than the one before it)

OR

where you can't use any words that contain the letter "e"?

Things to think about: Give it a try for as long as you can. Try to really communicate with either of the restrictions!

YOU MUST CHOOSE!

Would you rather live in the world of...

Final Fantasy **OR** Legend of Zelda?

Metal Gear **OR** Lego Indiana Jones?
If you could live in the world of one video game, what would you choose? Madden? Mario Brothers?

Who chose what game and why...

Name _____ Choice _____
Why _____

Name _____ Choice _____
Why _____

Name _____ Choice _____
Why _____

YOU MUST CHOOSE!

Chapter Seven

Would You...

Would you...? Could you...? Should you...? It's a simple "yes" or "no" question. That shouldn't be too hard, right? Guess again. It's time to find out what you're all about.

Would you... never speak to your brother or sister again to have free access to all video games and all movies?

Would you... want to look exactly like Ronald McDonald for $1,000,000?

Would you... have all your teeth surgically removed to have the strength of the Incredible Hulk?

YOU MUST CHOOSE!

Would you... drink poison ivy tea to get an "A" in all your classes?

Would you... use two-ply poison ivy toilet paper for a free trip to Disneyland?

Would you... rinse with poison ivy mouthwash to guest star on one episode of the TV show of your choice? What show would you choose?

Name of Show

_____

_____

Name of Person

_____

_____

YOU MUST CHOOSE!

Would you... bathe daily in a tub of nacho cheese to have $100 added to your allowance? Which of these would you bathe in for the $100:

Creamed spinach?

Prune juice?

Saliva?

Boogers, your own?

Boogers, from an elephant?

Would you... trade your house with your best friend's? Your wardrobe? Math skills? How about your jump shot?

YOU MUST CHOOSE!

What would someone have to give you for you to take a bite out of...

A four-year old Milky Way bar?

A stick of deodorant?

A dead mouse?

What's the grossest thing that you would take a bite out of ?

_____

For what? _____

YOU MUST CHOOSE!

Would you... drink a lint smoothie to be able to dunk for a day?

Would you... stick a live worm up your nostril for a twenty minute shopping spree at Toys Я Us?

Would you... consume a bag full of dead bugs for $10,000?

Would you... never miss a day of school for a year to be given front row tickets to an NBA championship game?

YOU MUST CHOOSE!

Would you... drink a glass of iced tea where the ice was frozen snot to never again catch a cold?

Would you... want to age at half the rate you currently age or not?

Would you... eat a Twinkie with a burrowing ant farm inside it to have the power to teleport for a day?

Would you... suck five live snails out of their shells for an *Iron Man* suit?

YOU MUST CHOOSE!

Would you... change your name to "Ahchoo" if you never had to go to school again? What about changing your name to "Butt-butt"?

Would you... want the power to be invisible if you always had a bad case of the farts when the power was activated?

YOU MUST CHOOSE!

Chapter Eight

Getting Personal

It's your turn to run the show. For the questions in this chapter, you may need to fill a blank with the name of a friend. Or maybe the name of an enemy. Or something else that only your demented imagination can conjure. Don't blame us for this chapter. It's your warped mind that's responsible for these deranged dilemmas.

Would you rather...

be teleported back in time to _____

(insert place and time period)

OR

have a pet _____?

(insert mythical creature)

Would you rather...

have poops that look exactly like

_____

(insert name of State)

OR

have farts that make the sound of

_____?

(insert sound)

YOU MUST CHOOSE!

Would you rather...

be taught in school by _____
(insert TV or movie star)

OR

be able to eat an unlimited amount of
_____ without getting sick
(insert food)

or gaining weight?

Take a vote!

Number of people who voted for choice #1: _____

Number of people who voted for choice #2: _____

YOU MUST CHOOSE!

Getting Personal

Would you rather...

have to hold hands with _____
(insert someone you don't like)
for one full day

OR

only be able to call _____
(insert teacher)
whenever using the phone for a week?

Would you rather...

have the power to change your face so that it looks exactly like _____
(insert celebrity)

OR

know the answer to any question you're asked related to _____ ?
(insert subject)

YOU MUST CHOOSE!

Would you rather...

appear as _____ whenever you
(insert cartoon character)

look in the mirror

OR

have the song _____ play whenever you
(insert song)

enter a room?

Would you rather live in a world where...

every Tuesday, it rained _____
(insert condiment)

OR

where _____ grew on trees?
(insert food)

YOU MUST CHOOSE!

Would you rather...

have lunch with _____
(insert athlete)

OR

_____ ?
(insert singer)

Would you rather...

make the sound of a/an _____
(insert animal)
when burping

OR

the sound of _____ when peeing?
(insert vehicle)

YOU MUST CHOOSE!

Would you rather...
have a huge tattoo of _____
(insert something silly)
OR
have a large _____ sprouting out of
(insert vegetable)
your back?

Would you rather...
be limited to wearing the same
_____ for the rest of your life
(insert article of clothing)

OR
listening to only one song, _____?
(insert song)

YOU MUST CHOOSE!

169

Would you rather...

be able to understand _____
(insert animal)
language

OR

have the ability to transform into

_____ **?**
(insert anything)

Who chose what and why...

Name _____ Choice _____

Why _____

Name _____ Choice _____

Why _____

YOU MUST CHOOSE!

Would you rather...

be a professional _____ **player**
(insert sport)

OR

_____ **?**
(insert awesome job)

Things to think about: If you could do anything, what job would you want?

Who chose what and why...

Name _____ Choice _____

Why _____

Name _____ Choice _____

Why _____

YOU MUST CHOOSE!

Chapter Nine

As Gross as it Gets

You could handle gross. You could even tolerate grosser than gross. But this is something different. This is a whole new league of gross. And remember, "I can't choose" is not an option.

Would you rather...

eat a slice of pizza seasoned with dandruff

OR

a slice of cake that you recently found behind your couch covered in dust and dirt?

Would you rather...

your parents serve you dinner off of dishes washed in toilet water

OR

sleep under a blanket of tent caterpillar nests?

YOU MUST CHOOSE!

WOULD YOU RATHER... EAT A HAMBURGER WITH A "SECRET SAUCE" THAT IS EAR WAX MIXED WITH MAYONNAISE

OR FRENCH FRIES THAT WERE DEEP FRIED IN SWEAT?

Would you rather...

lick clean one block of the New York City subway tracks

OR

scoop up some roadkill from the side of the road, bake it, and then eat it?

Who chose what and why...

Name _____ Choice _____

Why _____

Name _____ Choice _____

Why _____

YOU MUST CHOOSE!

Would you rather...

slide down a Slip 'N Slide covered in horse manure

OR

dive into a pool of tuna juice and stay in for 30 minutes?

Take a vote!

Number of people who voted for choice #1: _____

Number of people who voted for choice #2: _____

YOU MUST CHOOSE!

As Gross as it Gets

Grossed Out

Would you rather be sitting at your school lunch table and notice...

a 2-inch cockroach crawling on your plate **OR** a rat scampering across the floor?

hair mixed throughout your pasta **OR** a frog leg sticking out of your burger?

the cook mixing the iced tea with his unwashed hand **OR** that the expiration date on the milk you're drinking is 10 years old?

What's the grossest thing you've ever seen in your lunch room?

YOU MUST CHOOSE!

Would you rather...

have an ear ache, only to find out that a spider had laid eggs in your ear and the eggs were hatching

OR

have a stomach ache, only to find out that you have a parasite the size of a tennis ball living in your intestines?

Take a vote!

Number of people who voted for choice #1: _____

Number of people who voted for choice #2: _____

YOU MUST CHOOSE!

WOULD YOU RATHER...
ONLY BE ABLE TO EAT FOOD THAT IS 10 MONTHS OLD

OR ONLY BE ABLE TO EAT FOOD FROM THE TRASH?

Would you rather...
play bobbing for apples with rotten apples
OR
be caught in a hailstorm of eggs?

Would you rather...
gargle bleu cheese dressing every night instead of mouthwash
OR
wear liver-scented deodorant?

YOU MUST CHOOSE!

As Gross as it Gets

Would you rather...

eat bird beak "potato chips"

OR

petrified snake "pretzels"?

Would you rather...

wear a shirt made from fish skin **OR** shoes made from pig snouts?

earmuffs made from urinal pucks **OR** pants made from grease-drenched pizza plates?

_____ **OR** _____?
(insert your own)   (insert your own)

YOU MUST CHOOSE!

183

WOULD YOU RATHER... HAVE TO EAT A TUBE OF LIPSTICK EVERY MORNING FOR A WEEK

OR SHAMPOO WITH ELMER'S GLUE FOR A MONTH?

TUG
TUG
TUG

Chapter Ten

Random Play

Would You Rather...? **is on random play.** And when we say "random," we mean really RANDOM! There's no telling what kind of question will be asked: a curse, a torture, a power? And there's no limit to the obscenely odd, absolutely absurd, grotesquely gross situations you might be faced with.

Would you rather...

have 95 ribs **OR** 200 teeth?

have 2 left hands **OR** 2 left feet?

elephant's ears **OR** a baboon's butt?

Would you rather always have to wear...

clothes in the style of a 2 year old **OR** an 80 year old?

a stethoscope in your ears **OR** a scuba mask and snorkel?

a full New York Mets uniform **OR** an eye patch?

YOU MUST CHOOSE!

Would you rather...

get to rename other people whatever you want

OR

rename yourself whatever you want?

Who chose what and why...

Name _____ Choice _____

Why _____

Name _____ Choice _____

Why _____

YOU MUST CHOOSE!

WOULD YOU RATHER... EAT A SUNDAE WITH AN OLIVE FOR A CHERRY AND BROCCOLI INSTEAD OF NUTS

OR A "ZUCCHINI SPLIT" WITH KETCHUP INSTEAD OF HOT FUDGE?

Would you rather...
lose a tooth every time you sneeze
OR
gain a tooth?

Reasons 1st choice is better

_____

_____

_____

Reasons 2nd choice is better

_____

_____

_____

Would you rather...
fart the sound of a tuba
OR
hiccup the sound of a harmonica?

YOU MUST CHOOSE!

WOULD YOU RATHER...HAVE WEBBED ARMS AND LEGS

OR PERPETUALLY EXIST UNDER THE INTENSE GLARE OF A POWERFUL SPOT LIGHT?

WOULD YOU RATHER...HAVE EYELASHES THAT GROW AT A RATE OF ONE INCH PER MINUTE

OR HAVE HOT FUDGE PERPETUALLY DRIPPING FROM YOUR NOSTRILS?

Would you rather...

have a severe phobia of every angle other than 47 degree angles

OR

only be able to see people named Larry?

Things to think about: living in an oddly shaped room

Take a vote!

Number of people who voted for choice #1: _____

Number of people who voted for choice #2: _____

YOU MUST CHOOSE!

Would you rather...
take steps that are exactly 3 feet apart when you walk

OR

take steps that are exactly 3 inches apart when you walk?

Things to think about: _____

_____

_____

_____

YOU MUST CHOOSE!

WOULD YOU RATHER...ALWAYS HAVE TO WEAR NFL REFEREE GARB

OR A WIZARDS ROBE?

Would you rather...
be incapable of hearing people over the age of 20

OR

under the age of 20?

Reasons 1st choice is better

_____

_____

_____

Reasons 2nd choice is better

_____

_____

_____

Random Play

YOU MUST CHOOSE!

Would you rather...

your feet each weigh 15 lbs **OR**
your fingers each be 20 inches long?

your knees be as big as bowling balls **OR**
your elbows as big as softballs?

have neon orange eyes **OR**
wrinkles that wriggle like worms?

Would you rather...

soak in butter, then sit in the sun all day
OR
sandpaper your fingerprints off?

YOU MUST CHOOSE!

196

WOULD YOU RATHER...
BE ABDUCTED BY ALIENS AND PUT IN A ZOO EXHIBIT

OR BE STRANDED IN THE NORTH POLE?

WOULD YOU RATHER...HAVE FISH FOR HANDS

OR MOPS FOR FEET?

Fill in the Blank!
Would you rather...

your parents have a car whose paint job
features characters from _____
(insert cartoon)

OR

a car where the horn makes the sound
of a _____ ?
(insert sound)

Would you rather live
in a world...

where Teletubbies were a common species
of creature that lived in the wild

OR

where there were evil arch-enemy
versions of ourselves?

YOU MUST CHOOSE!

WOULD YOU RATHER...
LIVE IN A WORLD WHERE IT RAINED CARAMEL

OR IT SNOWED FROSTED FLAKES?

Would you rather...

be able to inflate your muscles to look strong, but have no actual exceptional strength

OR

be extremely strong, but have the body of a 90 year old?

Who chose what and why...

Name _____ Choice _____

Why _____

Name _____ Choice _____

Why _____

YOU MUST CHOOSE!

WOULD YOU RATHER...HAVE AN AFRO THAT GROWS WHENEVER YOU TELL A LIE

OR APPEAR AS ABRAHAM LINCOLN IN ALL PHOTOGRAPHS?

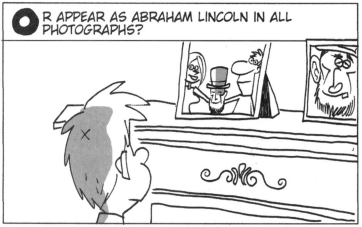

Chapter Eleven

Make Your Own Questions!

Okay, so you should have the hang of it by now. But do you have what it takes to write your own *Would You Rather...?* questions? Here's a hint: When in doubt, think weird, gross, embarrassing, cool, or painful. And don't worry; not only are there no wrong answers—in this case, there are no wrong questions!

Make Your Own "Gross" Question!
Make up two choices that are equally gross!

Would you rather....

_____

_____

OR

_____

_____ ?

Who chose what...

Name _____

Choice _____

Name _____

Choice _____

YOU MUST CHOOSE!

Make Your Own "Powers" Question!

Make up two choices that are equally gross!

Would you rather....

_____

_____

OR

_____

_____ **?**

Things to think about:

_____

_____

_____

_____

YOU MUST CHOOSE!

Make Your Own "Painful" Question!

Make up two choices that are equally painful!

Would you rather....

_____

_____

OR

_____

_____ **?**

Who chose what...

Name _____

Choice _____

Name _____

Choice _____

YOU MUST CHOOSE!

Make Your Own "Powers" Question!

Make up two choices that are equally gross!

Would you rather....

_____

_____

OR

_____

_____ **?**

Who chose what...

Name _____

Choice _____

Name _____

Choice _____

YOU MUST CHOOSE!

Make Your Own Question!

Make up two choices that are equally gross!

Would you rather live in a world where...

_____

_____

OR

_____

_____ ?

Things to think about:

_____

_____

YOU MUST CHOOSE!

Make Your Own "SUPER Gross" Question!

Let's see how disgusting you can be!!!

Would you rather....

_____

OR

_____ ?

Take a vote!

Number of people who voted for choice #1:

_____

Number of people who voted for choice #2:

_____

YOU MUST CHOOSE!

About the Authors:

Little is known about authors Justin Heimberg and David Gomberg. Some say they are locked up in a mental institution where they spend all day writing bizarre questions on their cells' walls. Others say they are aliens determined to confuse the planet into chaos. Still others say they are stricken with a bad case of "diarrhea of the imagination" for which no sort of toilet paper has yet been invented. If the last theory is right, look out! They say it's contagious!

About the Deity:

The Ringmaster/MC/overlord of the *Would You Rather...?* empire is "The Deity" (pronounced DEE-it-ee). It is the Deity who is responsible for creating and presenting the *WYR* questions, and it is the Deity who, without exception, proclaims **YOU MUST CHOOSE!** No one knows exactly why he does this. Suffice to say, it is for reasons beyond your understanding. Do not defy the Deity by saying "neither" or refusing to choose, or you may awaken to find yourself plagued with one of his horrible curses for real!

Got Your Own *Would You Rather...?* Question?

Go to www.sevenfooterkids.com
and submit your question and share it with
others. Read and debate thousands of other
dilemmas by the authors and other kids.

www.sevenfooterkids.com

Featuring:

New questions and illustrations!

More humor and games!

More funny game books!

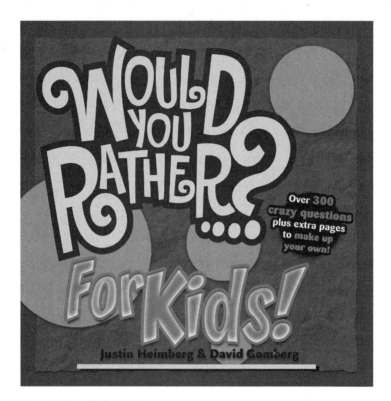

Would You Rather...? for Kids

The first book in the series written and designed for kids ages 8 and older, *Would You Rather...? for Kids* features hundreds of devilish dilemmas and imaginative illustrations! Kids will crack up as they ponder questions such as: **Would you rather...** have a tape-dispensing mouth *OR* a bottle-opening nostril?

www.sevenfooterkids.com